Lavonia Lusier-Bess

Reggie Bess: The Silent Player

...A mother's journey to raising a Deaf son

By

Lavonia Lusier-Bess

Edited by: Three Fold Cord Group, LLC

In Memory

In loving memory to Professor Virgil Carr, whom we will always remember for the impact he had on our son's life. Reggie was blessed for four years to have him as his accounting professor. Professor Carr taught him so much more that went beyond the books and classroom. Even today, Reggie patterns his classroom after him. Reggie will always cherish the mentoring, academics and friendship that he provided.

Dedication

This book is posthumously dedicated to Ms. Valerie Daniels for her signing, advocacy and commitment she provided Reginald Bess (Reggie) during his matriculation at Clark Atlanta University. Ms. Daniels signed for all his extra curriculum activities. There were many times she was called on to sign for his classes. Ms. Daniels was there for every beckon call. There were times she signed for him at Mt. Carmel Baptist Church.

Acknowledgements

There have been many people in my paths of life that have influenced me to write this book over the years and I would like to thank everyone for their support and belief in my abilities. I am extremely grateful for my supportive husband - Bill Bess; my children – Beverly, Lil Bill, Melba, and Reggie; and friends that have been there for me after God allowed me an opportunity to raise a child that was diagnosed as hard of hearing. Due to the large amount of people supporting me and my family throughout the years, I regret that I am only able to list a few of those that went above and beyond for me.

My sincerest appreciation goes to Ms. Linda Brown, Ms. Gloria Bivins (CAU employees), and Lisa White for all they have done for me. Ms. Brown and Ms. Bivins both made it possible for me to get in touch with different personnel at CAU. I had to call on them many times and they never failed to come to my rescue. There were times when I was lost for words and Ms. Brown would always get me on the right track and would always encourage me not to give up. Ms. White played an important part in Reggie's life after he graduated from college.

My gratitude is also extended to Ms. Carlita Booker-Tyler for interpreting for Reggie. Mr. James Booker was also instrumental by finding helpful resources in the deaf community.

I will always be indebted to Ms. Helen Risner from Clarkston High School. Ms. Risner provided a wealth of information on Deaf Culture and some personnel.

Thanks to Ms. Denise Sharif for introducing the recreational basketball opportunity which opened the door for Reggie to be open to playing basketball.

My gratitude goes to Ms. Martha Clark for gaining written approvals from parents of some of the deaf students for their individual letters to be published in this book.

Very special thanks for my youngest daughter, Melba Bess Goss for her assistance with her involvement with the final changes and providing great feedback and suggestions to finalize my first book. I appreciate my granddaughter, Naomi Barber for drawing the manual alphabet and "I love you" signs in sign language to be published in my book. I am also very appreciative of Takisha Foster for being a part of my life at the right time.

Contents

The Foreword

It is with great pleasure and pride that I write this introduction to my book. My intention for this book is to inspire other parents to get on the bandwagon and be a more integral support system for their children-especially the Deaf children. I certainly hope that you will understand some of the challenges that my son, Reggie, faced. He had so many wonderful, positive experiences that the negative aspect did not have an impact on him at all. Reggie was a very happy and jovial child growing up. There was never a disciplinary problem with him. He believed in following the rules and was very confused and disturbed to find out others were breaking the rules. As an example, in class one day, a student was trying to copy off his paper and he told the teacher. Also about two years after he had done a paper on Fibonacci, the mathematician, another student called and wanted to use his paper for their class project. He immediately said, "No! Do your own research." It has always been evident that Reggie was very serious about learning. Oddly enough, he did not want to go to college.

I thrived on the premise that it was paramount for all of my children to have an education, and that expectation includes Reggie as well. It was equally important to me, for Reggie to be self-sufficient. I wanted him to be able to survive without me since he was the youngest of four children. Reggie is very fortunate to have support and a background with education being the foundation in his family. I graduated from Dimery Business School and his dad, Bill, attended Fort Valley State University and served in the U.S. Navy. Beverly, the eldest, earned a Bachelor's degree in Mental Retardation and a Master's degree in Instructions; her husband, Herbert, has a Bachelor's degree in Business Management; William H. Bess, Jr., a retired service man that has a Bachelor's degree in Business Administration in Management; his wife, Irene, has a Bachelor's degree in Human Services in Management, two Master's degree, one in Education – Child Development, and one in Management; and Melba has a Bachelor's degree in Organizational Psychology and Development and working towards a MBA degree in Operations Management at American Intercontinental University (AIU). My goal was for Reggie to be as successful as his siblings. Additionally, I have four grandchildren who have graduated from college and one grandson, Jermaine, that has served with the United States Army. Jermaine's sister, Taylor, which recently graduated in the top ten percent from high school and their brother Montez is excelling in elementary school. Rachel Barber graduated from Georgia State University with a Bachelor's degree in Exercise Science. Her sister, Naomi, earned a Bachelor's degree in Commercial Design Art from Fort Valley and is currently enrolled in the MBA Program at Keller University. Latoya Bess graduated from Clark Atlanta University with a Bachelor's degree in Fashion Merchandising and received a Master's degree in Public Relationsand Communications from New York University. Her sister, Tijuana, recently graduated with a Bachelor's degree in Fashion Merchandising and Apparel Design Emphasis. Their sister Tahya is an honor student and taking college classes in high school. As I have made clear, education is taken very serious within my family, thus the motivation for pressing through the challenges in completing the writing of this book.

I worked for Clark Atlanta University (CAU) for twenty-seven years and Georgia Tech for three years. Unfortunately, my tenure ended at CAU in 2003. Reggie was a sophomore and was going to school on a CAU education tuition waiver. Inasmuch as I had worked for CAU for many years, this did not interfere with his matriculation. He was able to continue his education with the tuition waiver. However, it did put a damper on my enthusiasm about writing this book. I was working for Orkin Pest Control part-time and converted to a fulltime employee resulting in a diminished desire to write this book after leaving CAU. Fortunately, my passion to encourage other parents of children with impairments to fully understand the impact that remaining an active part of their child's educational, social, and physical development has on their success. This by far outweighed any challenges faced in completing this project. Although my hard of hearing son is now a full-grown adult living on his own, there is still more to look forward to in his journey. In fact, Reggie received his Bachelor's degree in Accounting, and minor in Math. He later earned his Master's degree in Deaf Education in December 2014. It is not confirmed, but Reggie is contemplating on getting his doctorate degree. What a chapter this will be!

My book was written to include factual details about the life of a son being raised as a child that is hard of hearing. Some of the characters and situations are factual and fictitious, and some may have been embellished for reading purposes.

I.

The Encounter

"Don't forget some oranges and some of that red juice Reggie likes, Lavonia!" Those were the words my husband Bill shouted as I headed out of the door. His request landed me in the busy grocery store with the longest lines I'd seen all season that day. As I pushed my cart towards the produce section of Winn-Dixie, I heard the sweetest, most innocent sounding voice asking for a banana. Approaching the bright red apples and the juiciest looking oranges in their barrels, I spotted the pair carrying on as if they were in the middle of making some serious life decisions. I laughed when I noticed the small voice was protruding from an even smaller body. She could not have been any older than two years old. Smiling broadly at this young wonder, I asked her mother the age of the beautiful little girl. "She is eighteen months old," the woman who looked to be in her late twenties, responded with a proud smile. "She is amazing!" I retorted with a smile. I had hoped that the worry circling my mind was effectively disguised by my grin. As she wheeled the cart away with her chatty, nearly two-year old in tow, I stood there with my hand still palming the last navel orange I was about to place in my sack. The encounter left me puzzled and slightly dismayed. My own child, Reggie, was already three years old, and had not yet spoken a handful of words. The knot in my stomach was increasingly making its presence known, but I could not move. My mind ignored the cue to shake the overwhelming curiosity. In hindsight, there were signs that something wasn't right.

Still, I refused to consider that Reggie was anything but a normal child. He was a normal, happy, hard-headed child.

The ride home from the grocery store after running all my errands was an overbearing one. The weight of my worries had overtaken my senses and my mind was all over the place. I began to retrace the events of the past four to five months in an attempt to remember when I noticed the first sign that my son, Reginald, needed some help. As my car wandered down the road, steered by an oblivious driver, my thoughts fought tirelessly down my path of memories covered during the most recent months. With the windows rolled down to invite the refreshing winds of the afternoon's breeze, I could hear the clatter of the neighborhood's adolescents and toddlers playing in the streets enjoying the cool weather. It was when I heard the voice of a concerned mother yelling after her child to stay clear of the cars driving down the road, that the event my mind searched for made its appearance in a daunting manner which served as the proverbial "light bulb moment."

My discovery that Sunday afternoon flashed across my mind as vivid as the blue sky that afternoon. Hurrying from church, I was anxious to get home and finish cooking the dinner I had begun preparing the night before. Reggie, left home with his father, was sure to be anxious to see me and receive the treat he knew I always carried in my purse for him. At fifteen months old, he was so jubilant and joyous. As I entered the house, I heard Bill calling my name to come into the living room. The anxious tone in his voice concerned me slightly, but nothing could prepare me for what he was about to uncover. “Lavonia, sit down,” Bill instructed as he placed Reggie in my lap. “I don’t think our son can hear, Lavonia,” he added with a distressed countenance. Positioning our child in my lap to face Bill as he stepped back away from us, he told me to call his name. Hopeful that my wonderful son would pass this quiz and discount his father’s apprehension, I called his name, “Reggie.” I spoke softly, bouncing him on my knee. No response. Raising my voice slightly higher, I repeated his name praying it would render acknowledgement in any form. For the second time, my son did not respond. My spirit was crushed, I turned Reggie around on my lap to face me and called his name a third time. Elated beyond expression that he responded this time, I held the fruit of my womb close to my heart, hugging him as tight as the first day he entered my life.

Reaching my driveway, I climbed out of the car pulling the grocery sack from the passenger seat. Mentally exhausted from recounting the scenes that transpired nearly a year and a half ago, I entered the house with a renewed determination. Placing the contents of the brown paper sack into the refrigerator, I headed towards the bedroom in search for Bill. I described to him the marvel I encountered at the grocery store and insisted that now was the time to forge ahead with getting Reggie's hearing tested again. Almost two years had passed since we visited his pediatrician who insisted we had nothing to worry about. I recalled him stating, "Einstein was six years old before he started talking." The reassurance he offered to ease our minds about Reggie's underdeveloped communication skills were now invalidated. At that time, he advised Bill and me that our son had fluid in his ear with an excessive amount of wax buildup that he would remove to alleviate the concern. The procedure required three of us to hold Reggie down while the doctor removed the wax, and it broke my heart to watch my child endure the torment. Following the medical procedure, Reggie would appear to be doing well, however, after a short time had elapsed, he would regress back to ignoring your call to his name. Motivated by witnessing the interaction with the young mother at the grocery store that day, I decided that enough was enough. Our persistence was proven fruitful. The doctor agreed to administer a psychological assessment as well as test his mobility. Additionally, he referred us to an ear, nose, and throat (ENT) specialist to examine our three year old. Following the doctor's instructions, we took Reggie to the ENT specialist who ultimately diagnosed him as being hard of hearing. He too, made a referral. He recommended that an audiologist review Reggie for a more specific prognosis. As any parent could imagine, the course of events left me disheartened. Having my child declared hard of hearing devastated me. Determined to have all possible options explored, Bill and I transported Reggie to the medical facility in the afternoon as requested by the clinician. He needed Reggie to be very tired and lethargic since he would connect him to a machine that measured sounds on his brain as he slept. The evaluation took three and a half hours and since my son refused to be alone, I was forced to hold him during the procedure. After analyzing the results, we were informed that the final professional diagnosis was that he was indeed hard of hearing. The measurement of sounds on his brain determined that Reggie could only hear low sounds and vowels. High sounds and consonants did not filter through his small ears. I was mortified. Immediately, I began to pray to God for wisdom, knowledge, and patience to handle this challenging ordeal.

Reflecting back to when I was thirty-nine years old and the doctor revealed that I was pregnant with Reggie, it was a very dark day for me. My oldest daughter Beverly, was a twenty-one year old junior at Morris Brown College and my oldest son, William Jr., whom we called Lil Bill, was thirteen years old and in the eighth grade. My youngest child at the time, Melba, was almost eleven years old and in the sixth grade, so to say that I was extremely disheartened about being with child at this point in my life would be an understatement. However, I acquiesced and eventually became thrilled with the idea of mothering a fourth child. Bill, my husband who was a dispatcher at Roadway Truck Lines, was ecstatic as well, especially since little Reginald Bess was born on his birthday, October 29, 1981. Reggie was a vibrant jovial baby. As he grew into a toddler, I noticed that he was becoming rebellious as the incidences of him failing to acknowledge our calls to him increased. I would have never guessed it to be an indication of my child being hard of hearing. Emotionally battered and mentally distressed, I sought consolation through my faith in God and my family. Calling on my sister, Juanita Buggs, who was living hundreds of miles away in Fort Wayne, Indiana, proved to be worthwhile as I made resolve and fortitude another mother would comprehend. Without delay, Juanita's reaction was to charge me with the mandate to assume primary governance of overseeing the ongoing care that would, from that point on, be the norm for both Reggie as well as the rest of our household. She recognized from the onset, that Bill would not be a primary active participant in ensuring that our son Reggie developed and progressed effectively as a "special needs" child. In her opinion, my husband's philosophy would be to allow whatever made our son happy to let him do it. I shared her speculation that his stance would leave Reggie at a developmental disadvantage, encouraging me to enthusiastically take her advice. The devastation, however, still did not subside. I was unsure of how to communicate with my son and was bewildered as to what I should do to care for him. Deciding to educate myself on the deaf culture would be paramount in guaranteeing Reggie's developmental and lifelong success, so I read what I could, but mostly relied on the guidance of his educators.

Dr. M. Clark recommended four schools for Reggie to attend. I chose to enroll him at Coralwood Learning Center when he was three years old and that began his matriculation in some form of an educational environment for all but four years of his thirty-three years of life. Reggie was mainstreamed throughout his entire education. Ms. Anne Rambo was his first teacher and set the stage for him to obtain a premium education. At Coralwood, Reggie acquired a firm foundation and received superlative instruction with a balanced measure of support and nurture. He later progressed to one of Coralwood's feeder schools to start kindergarten. Briarlake and Henderson Mill Elementary schools were both interested in Reggie attending their perspective schools. Ms. Mary Jenks, his teacher, took the initiative to call and confirm my decision to select Briarlake Elementary. I was so appreciative of all the guidance and support the teachers and administrators provided in the years following my decision. Ms. Polly Simpson, the Chairperson of the Deaf/Hearing Impaired Program at Briarlake, started priming Reggie for college by the time he reached the sixth grade. She encouraged the students to work vigorously, so by the time spring approached Reggie would be so tired that he did not want to go to school. Ms. Simpson often teased me by saying that Reggie was going to be a kindergarten dropout, but assured me that though the program was intense, the teachers would not overwork the students. In fact, it was during his tutelage at Briarlake Elementary, that Reggie was introduced to Charmaine Lewis. An English major in college, Charmaine worked for me in the Disability Services Program at Clark Atlanta University. When Reggie was in the sixth grade, Charmaine offered to assist him with a paper he had to write on 'Deafness'. She was so intrigued and fascinated by working with Reggie, that she subsequently pursued a Master's degree in Deaf Education when she enrolled at Columbia University for graduate school. A short time after enrolling, Charmaine made a trip back to Atlanta to monitor Ms. Simpson's class. Impressed by Ms. Simpson's teaching methods, it was shared with us that Charmaine decided to emulate what she'd observed in her own classroom one day.

Raising any child with special needs is a challenge, but I knew without a shadow of any doubt, in raising my hard of hearing son, ascertaining and implementing the most effective methods would be paramount in affording him adequate preparation to face the real world. It was of the utmost importance to both my husband Bill and I, to raise Reggie in a positive environment as well as in such a manner to encourage his security in his identity and his self-respect. We aimed to promote a positive self-image by any means necessary. Bill and I fully understood that effectively communicating with Reggie was going to be essential. It would be just as crucial for us to concentrate on our son's capabilities, rather than any of his inadequacies as a hard of hearing child. One of our primary objectives was to help Reggie to apprehend that the measure of his life was not characterized by his disability. On the contrary, his life would be rich and full of purpose. There are very high expectations Reggie's father and I had for all of our children-including him, so we were determined to be consistent instruments in his journey towards success. As his mother, I endeavored to be fully engaged in my attempts at educating myself about the impact of deafness on my son's learning and his language skills. I recognized the dire need to experience, from Reggie's perspective, the world around him. As he was physically connected to my world of hearing, it was pivotal for me to understand his deaf world.

II.
Just Imagine

Imagine for a moment trying to communicate all your feelings, emotions, and your most inner thoughts, without having the use of sound. How would you be able to do that? The obvious answer is communication. Though we take it for granted from time to time, communication is one of the greatest tools God has given us. The people of the Deaf community, though considered small, possess an inexplicable courage like no other. I have discovered, through time, they have taken what others would conclude to be a disadvantage and have turned it into being their greatest asset. Statistics show that two or three out of every one thousand children are either born deaf or hard of hearing. That is not a startling number to most. However, what I found to be alarming is that nine out of every ten children who are born deaf are born into families with parents who can hear. This could cause one to consider what a parent might experience emotionally or psychologically after discovering they have a child who has been born deaf or may have lost their hearing during the adolescent stage. Perhaps feelings of guilt would persist. Additionally, depression, and often fear of the challenges their child would already have to deal with before he or she can either learn how to stand or even walk, would plague their minds and hearts. As it relates to the arena of education, deaf children deal with many challenges. Some deaf youth only achieve a third grade reading level along with many other deficiencies in academics. Although there are many programs existing to help educate the Deaf, such as Individualized Education Programs (IEP), "without a strong command of language and an equally strong vocabulary, reading can be a painful experience for a deaf child," as identified by Ellen Risner- an administrator of the deaf/hard of hearing program at Clarkston High School where Reggie studied. Ms. Risner also noted that children and youth who are deaf or hard of hearing, have a more difficult time than normal hearing children learning vocabulary, grammar, word order, and other forms of verbal communication. The opportunity to lay the fundamental core for language presents itself very early and vacates swiftly, therefore, as I have discovered, it is critical for parents to educate themselves on the repercussion of being deaf on their child's communication, learning, and language. I am confident, as a result of my journey, that increased measures of educational and social success for deaf children can be assured amongst families where parents are a consistently integral part of their child's education from the onset. In addition to the very significant educational arena, sensitivity and cognizance of the social aspect of the deaf culture is just as essential. Socially speaking, triumphing over social immaturity can be one of the most paramount obstacles in parenting a deaf or hard of hearing child. In fact, deaf children are often found to be very reclusive within their own family environments.

III.

The Confrontations

"Mrs. Bess, I can certainly appreciate your situation, but it is of the most urgent importance that your young son gets the equipment as soon as possible." As he was moving his mouth the words began to slowly fade out. All I could think about was how I was failing my child. Certainly I understood how serious this situation was. Of course I realized that my son's life as well as my own had taken a very dramatic turn all at once. What I could not grasp, however, was how in the world I was going to pay for the hearing aids that would help my baby connect to my world and the world that surrounds him at every side. "Dr. Rosenburg, I know that Reggie needs these hearing aids right now, but our finances are overextended at the moment. My husband and I both work, but this unforeseen expense is just something that we cannot handle at the moment." I remember explaining through tears. I turned to Bill searching for a solution and noticed the same dread in his eyes. "Listen folks." Dr. Rosenburg continued, "discovering that your young son has lost his hearing is an experience I can definitely empathize with. Many of my patients have been hit with your same unexpected pain. Several of them are challenged with the financial constraints that you have shared with me today as well. However, I cannot stress the significance of young Reggie being fitted for hearing aids quickly. Are you able to borrow the money from any close friends or family?" The question stung like those swarm of hornets that attacked me that summer day near the hamburger spot my sister and I were standing outside of when I was a small child in Griffin, Georgia. There was no one in the family I could go to with such a burden. How could I even mouth my inability to take care of my son's need for a hearing aid? I had barely digested the painful truth that he was deaf. "Doctor, we have no extra money. I can't afford to get the hearing aids as you've suggested until I get my income tax refund check!" I replied in exasperation. As Bill turned to look at me with a puzzled countenance, I realized that my words were a bit abrasive. "I apologize, Dr. Rosenburg. Please understand that I am not irritated with you. I am just feeling helpless and vulnerable about this entire condition with my son. I am infuriated that he has to endure this and I confess that I am afraid that I do not fully comprehend how I am going to care for all of his needs." I continued with a softened voice. The car ride home was a teary-eyed emotional roller coaster. Thousands of thoughts ravaged my mind as we rolled down the expressway. The silence was thick until Bill turned to me and cut through the muted cries. "Lavonia," he stated, "everything is going to work out just fine." I recall him saying that afternoon. With everything inside of me I wanted to trust in my husband's confidence but I was afraid and shaken. With stubborn defiance, I fought against the thoughts of despair and sighed, "I know, Bill, you are right. Everything will work itself out." I am not sure if we were just trying to encourage each other that day or if we both truly believed in those statements, but time proved us correct sooner than we thought. Reggie's teacher, Ms. Anne Rambo, and his evaluator, Ms. Phyllis Harris, were very instrumental supporters in his early education. In fact, Ms. Harris very adamantly offered to buy the hearing aids for Reggie. "Ms. Harris, I appreciate the offer and Lord knows we need the help, but I'm not sure if I'm comfortable with the idea of you spending that kind of money on Reggie." I tried with all my might to decline her offer the morning we spoke about Reggie's visit with the audiologist when I dropped him off at school. Ms. Harris was always very concerned about Reggie and adored him as a student. "Now, Mrs. Bess, I know how difficult it can be accepting help from someone who is not a part of your family, however, your son has been like family to us here and if these hearing aids will help him excel here at school as well as in life, then I would like to do all that I can to help if that is all right with you," she countered. I conceded and agreed under the condition that she allow me to speak with my husband Bill first before making a concrete decision to accept her very generous offer. "Lavonia, I just do not see what the trouble would be in letting Ms. Harris help Reggie. How will his condition be affected if we waited until spring to buy the hearing aids?" Bill asked knowing that he was absolutely right. I knew he spoke the truth and waiting those few more months until spring would be unreasonable especially when we were being offered assistance. Two days later when I ran into Ms. Harris, I informed her that my husband and I had decided to accept her gracious offer to buy the hearing aids for Reggie. She smiled and hugged me tight, but for the life of me I could not fully understand why she was so excited about helping our son. “Mrs. Bess, my mind is completely set on making the purchase for the equipment Reggie needs to help him hear. I must tell you, however, that I did mention my intent to the school’s principal and he did not support my decision,” I stood back so that I could look into her eyes because I was unclear on what she was trying to tell me. With a soft chuckle Ms. Harris added, “but don’t worry, Mrs. Bess. I haven’t changed my mind. I can tell by the look on your face that my words were a bit perplexing. I merely mentioned it because I have even better news to share.” Ms. Harris continued to share with me that the principal did not want the staff to be so personally involved with the students and was against her financial support of Reggie. She quickly added that she was adamant about honoring her offer since it was her money that she had worked hard for and could spend any way she felt inclined. Subsequently, the principal, after realizing how determined she was in her stance, stated he would allow the PTA to purchase them. In hindsight, I’m sure that the broad smile that refused to be contained on my face, took Ms. Harris slightly off guard. I could not disguise how elated and blessed I felt that a group of people would be such a resource to my family. Reggie was so excited when he received the hearing aids. For a short while, he was even eager to wear them. His thrill was short-lived and he expressed that he was beginning to feel differently when one young lad started to make fun of him. I remember the day clearly. Reggie had run into the house and straight to his room. I could hear faint sounds of sobbing coming from his room so I made my way towards his bedroom door. Before I could reach the hall, I heard the door of the bathroom open and shut. Knowing that my son would not respond to my banging on the door, I began to stomp on the floor to signal that I was summoning him. That was our family's usual way of letting Reggie know that we were requiring his attention. Reggie opened the bathroom door with his head hanging toward the floor. I didn't notice it at first. Not until I took his hand and led him to the living room sofa, did I notice that his hearing aids were missing from his ears. Between his embarrassment and my escalating frustration, I was able to finally understand what he was trying to communicate. A neighborhood boy, 'Raymond' had taken his aids and hid them in the dirt between our house and the next door neighbors. Hurrying to put on my shoes, I hasten to get out of the door to inform Raymond's mother of his rude and unacceptable behavior. "Ma'am, I sincerely apologize for my son's behavior. This is not how I raised him to behave I can assure you," the short, portly woman who answered the door shrilled with a squeaky voice. The sound of children laughing and running throughout the inside of the seemingly neglected house made me certain that this woman had her hands too full to address the deviant behaviors of her son toward my child. If I had spoken those thoughts aloud I would have had to apologize. Barely thirty minutes later, my doorbell rang. As I opened the door, much to my surprise, was the same portly woman and her son. "What are you supposed to say, Raymond?" she quizzed, pushing the fragile looking boy towards where I stood in the doorway. Filled with apparent shame, Raymond took his eyes off the ground long enough to speak barely above a whisper. "I'm s-sorry, Miss. I was wrong to bother your son and I will make sure I find his ear things." I watched as he left my door post and walked to the patch of dirt between my house and the neighbor's. He got on his knees and dug into the dirt for almost five minutes before screaming with relief, "I found them! Here you go, Reggie. I found them!" We never had a problem with that Raymond boy again, nor did we have any concerns with Reggie's hearing aids being bothered. One of the obstacles in being a parent of a deaf or a hard of hearing child is combating issues regarding social maturity. Many deaf children experience challenges in "fitting in." Consequently, the deaf child or adolescent can be more inclined to becoming a victim of a bully. As a result of missing out on what could be considered normal verbal connections, the opportunities to comprehend clues or signals of facial expressions or body language that often allude to deviant or negative behavior patterns seem to escape a deaf child. This is probably the reason I was so grateful that Reggie eventually formed a bond with two other young boys in the neighborhood. Garland Jairrels and Raymond became two of my son's best friends. Though the pair could hear, they remained closely connected to Reggie for many years. To this day, I commend them for the love, protection and concern they maintained for Reggie. I had named them "The Notorious Three" because when you saw one, you saw them all. Reggie also had a very close bond with another hard of hearing young man, Victor Calloway, in which I strongly believe, taught Reggie how to relate with other youth who were not deaf.

Reggie's social challenges did not end with bullies or even any concerns at school. When Reggie was five years old, he had gotten so bored with going to church. There was no interpreter and all he did would scribble on the Sunday service program that the ushers handed out each week. One day, after I realized I could not continue just sitting idle in this concern of mine, I had a talk with Pastor Timothy Flemming. Reverend Flemming agreed to hire an interpreter for Reggie. He hired Ms. Carlita Booker and Tracie Davenport. They both did an excellent job. Ms. Zadie Long graciously volunteered to sign and did extremely well. Reggie was very blessed to have had great interpreters. Ginny Bowling and Keith Smith aided Reggie with sign interpretation from elementary school through college. The law states that the schools have to provide certified interpreters for all Deaf students. Several Disability Coordinators in college stop at that. Reggie explained to me that there is not a sign for every word. Therefore, the interpreters and the students on many occasions have to make their own signs for some words. I can't convey to you how important it is for the interpreter and the student to learn new signs for words together and have a genuine understanding to signing.

IV.

Circles of Life

Reggie did not allow the fact that he was hard of hearing to prevent him from participating in different activities, such as basketball. He played forward for the varsity basketball team at Clarkston High School. Reggie was at the foul line about to make his first of two free throws to either tie or win the game. He bounced the ball a few times before he picked it up to shoot. The visiting team was screaming and yelling while waving banners and such, trying to break his concentration. All of his siblings, with me included, were at the game, watching with joy knowing that Reggie was going to make the two shots with ease. I reached over to my husband and said, "I don't know why they are screaming because he can't hear them." We both chuckled as if we knew a secret that no one in the audience knew. Reggie's attempt at the first shot was successful and the crowd grows silent. The referee grabs the ball and makes a gesture signaling to the kids that this is the last shot. The crowd begins screaming again, but Reggie is still poised and focused. It was obvious he was more than confident that he was going to make the game-winning shot. He shoots the ball and it was like slow motion how the ball went up into the air, bounced on the rim, only to fall directly into the net. The visiting team was left stunned from what just happened. The home team, along with some members of the crowd ran toward Reggie with joy because they had won the State Championship. Reggie, showing no emotion, comes from under the crowd and heads toward the locker room while the rest of the team celebrated their long, hard fought victory against a formidable opponent. I was always happy about Reggie's perseverance in getting things done. No matter the task, Reggie was always determined to get the job finished. As we were getting ready to meet him in the locker room to take him home, Lil Bill jumped up from the seat and darted towards the locker room shouting, "I'll see you guys there." Before my husband or I could even stop him, Lil Bill was gone. Reggie and Lil Bill were very close. Though they were a few years apart, you could not tell because of how they spent so much time with each other. Reggie exits out of the locker room and he notices his big brother. Instantly, a look of joy comes over his face. Lil Bill gives his younger brother a hug and a high-five for his recent accomplishment. When I reached the pair, watching my children interact with each other, was more rewarding than anything else in the world. It was a surprise to us all when the younger Bill came home the night before on a week long pass from the Army. Though I could barely contain my excitement at seeing him walk through the front door, Reggie was more elated than the three of us combined. As if reading my mind, Reggie runs to me, gives me a hug and looks into my eyes. The brief, yet intense stare we shared calmed me. It was as if Reggie told me without speaking, that we are going to be ok. I kissed him on his forehead and squeezed him tighter, letting my son know how proud I was of him. “Come on, let's go! I'm hungry!”

said Bill in a rush to leave the venue. Memories of Reggie began racing through my mind as we walked out together through the double doors into the parking lot. Finally, my thoughts settled on a few years prior when I was sitting at the table with Reggie trying to help him with his math homework. He would present the problem to me and we would write it out together. We had spent hours solving problem after problem until he went to bed. Even after he was fast asleep, I stayed awake studying his assignment just to make sure that every problem was right for his math class. The next day, my daughter Melba and I were sitting at the kitchen table preparing for dinner when we heard the front door slam and someone running upstairs. Another door slammed again. I ran into the living room trying to figure out the commotion. I discovered Reggie's book bag halfway unzipped with his math homework hanging slightly out and resting near the stairs. There was a bright red 'F' on the front page. In disbelief, I scooped up his book bag along with his homework to make sure that it was indeed an 'F' on his assignment. "Melba, come look at this please." I called out into the kitchen where I had left her. "Please tell me that my eyes aren't deceiving me!" I pleaded, growing more concerned by the minute. Melba took the paper and I stomped on the carpeted floor for Reggie to come down stairs. He could hear low sounds, such as stomping the floors, and knew that he was being summoned. Reggie stood at the top of the stairs with his arms folded. The look on his face told me that his world was crushed. I raised my arms in a hug formation to signal him to come down stairs. "This is wrong, momma," he blurted shaking his head, "this is wrong!" Melba turned to me and agreed. "Momma, Reggie is right. All of the math problems are wrong. Come here, let me show you" she offered, motioning him to come down the stairs. Watching Reggie and Melba sit in the living room and go over every problem I completed in error, I looked at my son stunned because for the first time I failed him. This was one of many lessons that I learned about him. He never asked me again to help with homework, yet he became more independent on making sure that he got things done. His math teacher, Ms. Stephenson, explained to him that in order to do math, he had to understand math.

"Lavonia, did you want the buffet or the specialty pizzas?" I had almost forgotten that I was standing in the middle of the pizza restaurant we often frequented. "The buffet is fine Bill." I replied as I was still traveling down memory lane thinking about my children. Reggie was sitting at the table while Melba, Lil Bill and Beverly went to get some pizza, salad, and pasta from the buffet. I sat next to Reggie and held his hand. The atmosphere of the pizzeria was a very festive one. Children and adults were either getting their food or playing video games. It gave me a warm feeling inside knowing that my family was having a good time with each other. I noticed, however, as I was walking to the table, my son didn't really seem interested in eating. Reggie was normally the type to keep to himself, but his countenance signaled that something was wrong. I sat in front of him and looked into his big brown eyes. "Are you ok?" I signed looking for the confirmation that everything was all right and that he was just waiting for me to come near. He nodded his head and turned away looking out of the window. It was moments like those where I wished that I could read his mind in efforts to try to find some way to connect with him on a deeper level. Just then, my husband comes to the table with a plate full of pizza and salad. "Lavonia, go ahead and get you something to eat before the food gets cold," I recalled him saying, "Reggie will be ok," he added prodding me to leave my son's side. “I'm just going to sit here for a while, Bill. I am not hungry.” I would decline to no avail. “Sure you are,” Bill retorted as he placed his hand over mine. His face showed that he understood. Bill was always there to say the right words to take my mind off of the everyday struggle and just enjoy the simple things in life. As Lil Bill and Melba returned to the table, Reggie's face instantly lit up full of joy as if he just woke up on a snow-filled Christmas day and received the perfect Christmas present he had been asking about for a very long time. Lil Bill seemed to have inhaled one slice of pizza when he looks to me and asks, "Momma, I'm going to take Reggie over to the basketball video game to win some tickets, is that ok?" Reggie read his lips and looked over toward the back of the pizzeria and saw the basketball hoop and looked to me tapping my hand and pointing to the game as well. How could I deny him knowing that this time with his big brother was going to keep him entertained? I grabbed a slice of pizza off my husband's plate and handed it to him. "Eat this and you can go." I agreed handing him a napkin as well. He took two bites of the pizza and smiled. We all chuckled as I told Lil Bill to keep an eye on Reggie before they went to the back of the restaurant. Reggie loved basketball. Sometimes, when I got home from work late I would have to go to his friends' house around the corner to pick him up because he was so competitive. On one occasion, he was so upset that he could not shoot a lay-up, that he would practice without end until he mastered the shot. Moving down the buffet line looking for some pizza, I watched the boys play the basketball game from my peripheral vision. Lil Bill was better at shooting the ball than Reggie was, so they would continue to play that game until they both grew exhausted. This was one of many moments that I would always cherish. The dark day of discovering I was pregnant again at the age of thirty-nine had turned into the brightest years of my life. My children were an essential part of my sanity. They meant more to me than the very air I breathed. I was determined that our lives as a family would be a direct reflection of my upbringing in my loving home as a child. When I was growing up, we were very poor but we had an abundance of love for one another.

I was born in Griffin, Georgia to a sweet, mild, and loving woman-the late Pauline Lusier, and my father-the late Thomas Lusier. To say we were poor would be a tremendous understatement. We lived in a two-room house. That's right! A two-room house where there was a bed placed in the kitchen so that everyone could have a place to sleep. Though crowded with nearly-bare pantry shelves, I remember that home being full of love. The surrounding dirt roads and the misshapen door frames would attempt to tell a different story, but my siblings and I were grateful for the memories shared with each other along with our devoted mother. Hoping to offer my share and financially contribute to the small amount of money and food with which my mother was able to supply our home, I began working at the age of eleven for a prominent white family. Joyce and Frank Thomas had agreed to let me work permanently in caring for their three children-Bob, Frank, and Beverly. I played with them and kept them entertained while my sister, Hessie, would do the cooking and cleaning. Even today, Frank Jr. chuckles about the time I tried to teach him to dance when he was five years old. I grew to love this family remarkably. As a matter of fact, I named my eldest daughter, Beverly, after Mrs. Thomas. There were some nights when I would stay over because I was both excited and curious about their way of living. Although it was sort of a culture shock for me, I had learned so many useful lessons from Mrs. Thomas. During the staunch period of segregation, she and Mr. Thomas provided me with a wealth of knowledge regarding diversity. Their actions would come to speak volumes over empty words and I was grateful that this family had opened their arms, heart, as well as their home to me. They trusted me to care for their children, and often would allow me to accompany them to her friends' homes for birthday parties and sometimes just to play. This would eventually shape my vision and fuel my hope that one day I could have some of the nicer and finer things in life as they did. The Thomas', as I observed, always supported their children and kept them active in all kinds of activities. This definitely helped me to develop into the loving and supportive mother that I have strived to be for my children and my family. Along with the overwhelming love I received from my own family, spending so much time with the Thomas family served as a beacon of light as to how life could be for me one day. It planted a seed that I still carry today as it concerns encouraging and supporting my own children. The great advice, physical and financial assistance, and welcoming arms I received whenever needed, kept me close to Mr. and Mrs. Thomas long after I finished high school and eventually business school. Until they both were deceased, the Thomas' and I stayed in touch. I am indebted to them as I now watch my own family.

I never thought I would comfortably adjust to being the parent of a deaf child, but here I stood watching Reggie with his older siblings. Amongst them, he was still as vibrant as he was when he was a toddler. He absorbed all of the love they continued to pour out on their youngest brother. With meal time just about over, Bill, Melba, the boys, and I headed home to my house that evening where we would sit and listen to Lil Bill share stories of his time in the Gulf. It was no secret that Reggie idolized his brother, and sitting around the living room that night made it clearer. When my son, Lil Bill, was initially deployed to the Gulf, Reggie had a very difficult time grasping the reality that his older brother would be gone for some time. As best as I tried, I did not know how to explain it to him in a way that he could understand. The significance of Lil Bill's absence from Reggie's life prompted him to search for understanding on his own. I remember the day he came home from school very excited to let me know that he now understood what the war was all about. That was another indication as to how independent a thinker Reggie would become.

Reggie was captivated by learning. He was so inquisitive and never stopped asking questions. He continued to do very well in school as well as recreational basketball, even participating in various extracurricular activities and programs. Reggie's father, Bill, was extremely committed with his support of our son's participation in the sports programs. Reggie started playing recreational basketball at the age of eight. Every summer, the team would go to Central Florida for a week to participate in a tournament. So every year, we turned it into a family vacation and thoroughly enjoyed the getaways. To help with the expenses of the trip, Bill would always work a second job providing lawn care services. Though he and I both thought it would be best for our son to ride and interact with the team in route to the tournaments, Reggie did not want to ride the bus with the team nor sleep in the rooms that were assigned for the players. He despised being different from everyone else, but agreed to remain with the team. It never dawned on Bill and I, that this would be such an experience for him and that one day he would become a coach as well as an Athletic Director. During his school years, Bill went to every practice and remained on site until each practice was over. This would include Reggie's time playing on the Junior Varsity team in middle school as well as the Varsity team during high school. There was a time when Bill was at Reggie's basketball practice when Reggie and a few players were trying to learn the three-man weave play. Reggie was captivated by learning. However, on this day, it seemed as if that Reggie just couldn't understand the format of the play and he kept missing the time to catch the ball or pass the ball. The newer players on the team laughed at Reggie, making fun of him by cracking jokes and pointing, while most of the older players began to defend Reggie, encouraging him to keep going. With all of this going on in the gym,

Reggie became embarrassed and it caused him to become bothered so he walked over to the bleachers to have a seat in the middle of the play. Bill noticed the kids teasing his son. It was during this encounter, that Bill asked his then coach, Eric Lawson, if he could speak with the team. Coach Lawson agreed and Reggie was clueless as to what his father would possibly have to communicate to his teammates. "Sure, you can speak to the team. I have some things to tell them myself!" says the coach reaching for the whistle in his pocket. "Hey!!! Everybody gather around half court. We need to have a talk." Coach Lawson orders the team making them form a circle. Bill motioned for Reggie to meet him in the middle of the circle along with his coach. Reggie didn't want to disrespect his father by not going to meet him, so he slowly got up from the bleachers and walked over. Once there, Bill placed his hands on Reggie's shoulders and stood behind him. "The floor is all yours, sir." Coach Lawson motioned to Bill. "Thank you, Coach Lawson." Bill nods as he looked into the eyes of each and every teammate in the circle making sure that he has their undivided attention. "Listen up, guys," Bill started, "Reggie has a voice and he can talk. I want you fellas to include my son in on your conversations," he continued. "In order for this team to work, everybody must learn to communicate with each other. Can you guys do that for me?" he quizzed the group. "YES SIR!!!!" the team shouted in unison as if they were ready for battle. Reggie observed the countenance of his teammates and saw the remorse on their faces for taunting and laughing at him. Coach Lawson blew the whistle to regain their attention. "Now, it's my turn to talk," he stated, "and I'm going to be brief. I need twenty laps around the gym and fifteen pushups. Reggie, since you walked to the bleachers in the middle of the play you only have to do five laps," he concluded by turning in Reggie's direction to face him. Reggie looked at his father hoping that he would be able to get out of this and Bill motioned Reggie to go along with the rest of the team. On the way home after practice, Reggie sat in the back seat looking out of the window while Bill listened to the radio enjoying the music trying to take his mind off of the events that happened at basketball practice earlier. My husband always wanted our son to live and play like every other child. He often grew frustrated when Reggie was not being treated equally by others, whether if it were family or not. He looked through the rearview mirror and watched his son gazing out of the window. "I love you son, and I'm going to do everything that I can to make sure that no one will make you feel different," he mouths to himself in the mirror. Suddenly, Reggie reached over the back seat and touched his father's right shoulder and squeezed. It reassured Bill that Reggie had read his father's lips and responded to him. Overwhelmed by the emotion from his son, Bill let his left hand go from the steering wheel and placed it on Reggie's hand. The silent but impactful moment between the two of them showed that though they may not communicate that often, his son appreciated what he did for him in the gym. Tears fell from Bill's eyes as they journeyed home that evening, he later confessed to me, "It's going to be okay, son. We are going to be okay." Reggie takes his hand off of Bill's shoulder and displays a really big smile and places both thumbs in the air causing Bill to smile at his son. Bill held up his right thumb and said, "We did it son! We did it!" It was just what was needed to break the sentimental moment between them two. When Bill shared this with me that evening, I was so proud of my husband. He happily divulged the new name he had given the team for Reggie that afternoon. “The Silent Player” Bill whispered with a wide smile in his face as we sat in the bedroom. “I like that. The Silent Player really fits him, huh Bill?” I smiled back that night.

Reggie was someone who would never let his disability become a challenge to him ever in life. Sometimes I would chuckle when I think about the time Bill and I taught Reggie how to drive. Reggie used to always grab the keys and make his way to the driver seat of my car each and every time I would grab my coat and purse. Sure he was old enough to drive, however I was a bit skeptical at first with the thought of him driving anyone's car, let alone my own. So I would just have Reggie ride with me on the weekends to the store or any other errands that I would be handling at the time. But it never stopped Reggie from grabbing the keys and heading to the driver seat to somehow show me that he can drive the family car. His moment of truth came one morning when we were running late for church. We were all rushing around the house and I was really tired because I was up most of the night working on the Sunday school lesson for the kids. Like clockwork, Reggie was already dressed and ready to go. He gets downstairs and grabs the car keys from the kitchen table and got to the car. My husband Bill sat in the living room, peacefully waiting for me to come downstairs and tear into Reggie because of his disobedience. "Lavonia, come into the living room for a moment please. I need to speak to you for a moment," he requested. "I'm in a rush, Bill," I mentioned in with a huff, "Reggie has grabbed my keys again!" Bill smiled and tapped his hand on the couch pillow next to him. "That is actually what I wanted to talk to you about. Please baby, come sit down. There is something that I want to share with you." As I walked towards my husband, a multitude of questions swam through my head, trying to figure out what else has happened to my child. Bill placed his hands over my hand and kissed me on the cheek. "Lavonia baby, I have a confession to make to you. Sometimes when you're coming home from work late, me and Reggie would take the car out for a spin around the neighborhood so that I could teach him how to drive." I was stunned by the news that my husband knew all of this and didn't inform me. "Bill, are you telling me that you have been teaching Reggie how to drive?" I quizzed. "Yes!" he confesses, continuing to show me his pearly white smile. "Now, I know that you are running late and you have to get to church, so I'll make a deal with you. I'll sit in the front with Reggie while he's driving and if he makes any sharp turns or swerves the car making you uncomfortable in any way, I'll stop the car and I'll drive the rest of the way to church. Is that ok?" he asks. I agreed because we were already running late and I just wanted to get to Sunday school before the other kids got there. Reggie and his father had a system going on where he would tap Reggie's leg once to go, tap twice to stop, place one finger on the dashboard to go left and two fingers to go right. It was remarkable to watch Reggie and his father communicate with each other in this manner. I was so fascinated by this, that I actually wasn't nervous at all about Reggie driving the car. Thank God we made it on time to church.

V.

Transitions

One evening while I was preparing dinner for the family, I noticed some mail at the dinner table. Maybe it just slipped my mind I guess, since I just got home from work trying to decide what side dishes would accompany the chicken already baking in the oven. "Melba, did you tell me that there was some mail at the table?" I mumbled to myself as I walked over to the round, glass table pondering what bills we needed to pay. To my surprise, I noticed not only one, but three letters from colleges were addressed to Reggie. Instantly I became overjoyed and rushed to open the correspondence to view its contents. "Reggie is going to love this," I stated with glee scanning over the information about the colleges and what they had to offer. Just then, Reggie walked through the door coming in from playing basketball outside with his friends. He kisses me on the cheek to greet me and I grabbed his hand to motion him to sit down. Trying to decipher the look on my face, my son places his hand on mine. "What's wrong, mama? Are you ok?" Shaking my head to confirm, "Yes, I'm ok baby. I want you to take a look at this and tell me what you think about it." I responded as I slid the literature to him, smiling to myself feeling grateful that my son had reached this pivotal moment to decide the next chapter in his life. He had matriculated through high school, achieving all sorts of recognition from his peers as well as educators at the schools he attended. For a moment, I saw myself and Bill at one of his college basketball games cheering for our son as he makes the winning shot, or preparing a meal for him as he came home to study for one of his mid-week exams . My mental journey with my son came to a screeching halt when he made the oddest declaration when he declared, "Mama, I don't want to go to college, but this is nice." Multiple questions ran through my mind like a flood trying to figure out how or even why he came up with this decision to not go to college and further his education. "Why is it that you don't want to go to college, Reggie?" I asked hoping to get an alternative answer. He adamantly replied, "Mama, I just don't want to go to college. I'm done with school right now." His answer didn't satisfy my curiosity, so as I was about to ask another question to find out more about his decision, my husband Bill walks through the door.

Timing could not be more perfect for Reggie as he shot from the table and darted up the stairs before I could get his attention. "We will talk about this later!!" I yelled before he shut the door to his room. "Who's that lady..." sings my husband taking off his jacket placing it on the hook on the back of the door. "What's going on, baby? How was your day?" Bill questioned with a smile. I rose from the table to meet him with a kiss and a hug and proceeded to finish dinner. "It was good. The dinner is almost done. We are having baked chicken with mixed vegetables over some brown rice." Bill went to the kitchen table to have a seat and watched me as I moved from the refrigerator to the stove. "Sounds good to me, my love!" He would always tell me how he loved to watch me cook because I would be so focused and put so much love into my food. "So...who's going to college, Lavonia baby?" I poured the bag of mixed vegetables in the pot and answered, "Reggie got this in the mail today and before you came in, we were talking about it." Bill scans the documents and smiles. So he's excited about going to college, right?" I didn't want to change my husband's happy disposition, but he needed to know the truth. I opened the oven to check the baked chicken and stirred the pot of veggies while setting the stove to simmer. "Well, babe," I responded to Bill with a sigh, "Reggie doesn't want to go to college. He told me that he is tired of school." Bill gathered up all of the mail from the kitchen table and placed it on the shelf next to the back door. Though he graduated from high school, he still has to figure out what he wants to do with his own life. So let's give him that time." I went back to the stove to finish up the veggies and rice and took the chicken out of the oven. Though I understood what my husband was trying to convey, I just didn't want my son to just stop at high school when I know he could handle college. Dinner was ready and we called Melba and Reggie down so that we could all eat together. I didn't mention college at all because I believed that at the dinner table was where we should be at peace. Yet the conversation of both my husband and my son kept repeating in my mind. Even when I went to bed, I just couldn't sleep because I was completely consumed with thinking about what Reggie would decide to do now that he's graduated from high school.

Throughout his tenure at Clarkston High School, Reggie had two of the greatest influences in his high school academics. Ms. Ellen Risner and Ms. Elizabeth Fox were both very instrumental in my son's educational success. During our initial meeting, Ms. Risner informed me that she would place Reggie in a group that would keep him so busy that he would not have time to do anything but school work. Subsequently, Reggie was placed in some advanced courses and ultimately, he was taking all the advanced classes that were offered to him. It became critical that I consistently interacted with the administrators behind the scenes and I learned to implement exactly what they advised. Though he was extremely challenged and struggled with his English course, Reggie was committed to succeeding and worked very diligently to excel. Recognizing that his struggle was due to my son having a difficult time understanding the assigned tasks because he could not clearly comprehend the instructions, I spoke to the instructor who admitted that this was the very first time she had ever taught a deaf person. She, however, offered to work with Reggie after school. With English being his second language, her sacrifice provided Reggie with excellent support. He grew even more determined to exceed the academic expectations of both his teachers as well as his family. There were evenings where Reggie would stay up extremely late studying on working on assignments. His focus became so intense that he once awakened at four o' clock in the morning to do homework because he thought it was a school day-only to discover that it was a Sunday. The intensity of his focus finally outweighed his joy of even playing basketball.

While in the twelfth grade, Reggie decided that he would only concentrate on academics and not play basketball anymore. The choice was his alone and I was shocked. Determined to improve his grade point average (GPA), his focus paid off. His GPA had improved to a 3.6 and for two consecutive years, Reggie was nominated to *'Who's Who Among High School Students'* and the National Honor Beta Society. He was even awarded with the highest recognition at his school for academic excellence-The Presidential Award. To say that my husband Bill and I were extremely proud of his accomplishments in the classroom would be an understatement for sure. His academic achievements in the classroom did not reflect onto his standardized testing. Reggie's first attempt at taking the Scholastic Aptitude Test (SAT) did not fare well. As a result, Reggie attended the Urban League SAT workshop. I was very much discontented after learning that they would not provide an interpreter for him and he was reluctant to attend as well. However, Reggie participated in the workshop for a period of four Saturdays before attempting the SAT again. His participation proved effective and his scores improved tremendously.

Although content with the results of his second attempt at the SAT, Reggie was far from concerned with going to college. He had no idea what he would major in, however, his administrators Ms. Risner, Ms. Fox, and myself all decided that the only option Reggie had was to attend college. Collectively, we had discussed that since Reggie was good with numbers perhaps that was what he should major in. Ms. Fox had previously informed me that one of Reggie's classmates was enrolled in Perimeter College majoring in Accounting and doing well. Liberal Arts courses would present difficulty, as we agreed, so Accounting courses would be the path for Reggie. When I got everything together for him to just sign the papers to enroll, we sat at the table to discuss it. Reggie was resistant at first, but we agreed that if he doesn't like college after a semester then he can quit all together. After graduating from Clarkston High School, Reggie enrolled at Clark Atlanta University (CAU). Reggie was truly blessed to have so many great outstanding professors at CAU. Following his enrollment, Dr. Phillips, the Chairman of the Accounting Department, called and informed me that Reggie was a natural-born mathematician. Dr. Phillips would continue to ensure that my son would have the tutelage of the best professors in the department. He assigned the late Professor, Virgil Carr for his entire matriculation at CAU. Professor Carr, in my opinion, was one of the best professors that anyone could have at any University. He nurtured and helped build Reggie's self-esteem. He was a perfect role model for Reggie. Although Reggie did not pursue his career in accounting, the principles that he taught him has tremendously helped him at his present occupation. Despite the great molding by Professor Carr, however, Reggie had some struggles at CAU also. There was one professor who had never taught a hard of hearing/deaf person before. It was evident that she felt overwhelmed and as a result, was very adamant that she did not want Reggie in her class. She indicated that having an interpreter in the classroom would be a distraction for the class. That issue was soon resolved and he was able to maintain his grades in the class. There was another challenge in one of his other classes as well. Reggie did not do well on one of his exams so the professor talked to the interpreter about his not faring well in the class in the presence of all his classmates. Of course, Reggie left very frustrated and upset, to say the least. The Disability Service Coordinator wrote a letter to the Dean and the matter was resolved.

After completing nearly two years of his secondary education at CAU, Reggie decided that accounting was not what he wanted to pursue. As a result, he reached out to the Associate Dean of the Business School, Ms. Juanita Carter, who encouraged him to continue with his major in Accounting and include Mathematics as a minor in his studies. He complied with her advice and graduated with an Accounting major and a minor in Mathematics. In fact, while still enrolled at CAU, Reggie tutored math at Georgia Perimeter College. Reggie attempted to work in other arenas; however, mathematics was where his passion remained. Therefore, following graduation, he continued tutoring the subject of math. During one summer, Reggie attempted to venture out in efforts to obtain monetary sustenance by working for Fed Ex. It lasted for only three weeks as Reggie considered the work to be extremely difficult and strenuous and could not sustain the level the energy it required. I constantly encouraged him to remain employed since he didn't have any other means of income during the summer months while he was out of school, however, he did not. "It's too much! I can't do it!" I recall him exclaiming with a pained countenance one summer afternoon when I returned home from work. Entering the house with my keys still in hand, I found Reggie standing in the kitchen with the refrigerator door wide open as he sipped on a glass of fruit juice. He almost immediately noticed the puzzled look on my face when approached the space where he was standing. Hastening to explain the reason he was at home instead of at work with Fed Ex, he quickly closed the refrigerator door and held his hands up as if to signify surrender. Deep down, I knew the strenuous tasks he would be required to complete would prove difficult for my son, especially since he was at a disadvantage because he could not hear daily instructions from management. However, I desperately desired for him to learn how to be financially self-sufficient while he was out of school during the summers. Despite my persistent encouragement to remain employed, Reggie spent every summer with limited employment. "I just don't know what else to say or do, Bill." I shared with my husband one evening while home alone. I had grown nearly exasperated at my futile attempts to help our son with obtaining income while at home. "Just leave the boy alone, Lavonia, I am sure our young man will figure it all out on his own," my husband would caution. I found that easier said than done, but I complied with Bill. Secretly hoping that his convictions would prove true, I withdrew for a time and allowed Reggie to determine the best recourse in securing income while away from school during his summers.

Furthering his passion for mathematics and complimenting his endeavors in tutoring math after completing his undergraduate studies, Reggie began working as a teacher. According to the guidelines set for Georgia educators, until he obtained proper certification, operating as a teacher would be his only option. Consequently, the family and I urged Reggie to take the Georgia

Assessments for the Certification of Educators (GAYCE test). If I recollect accurately, there were three parts to the examination-two of which he eventually passed. The third part, however, proved to be a goliath of a task for Reggie to score sufficiently. He had taken the first and second parts of the GAYCE test numerous of times and had almost surrendered to quitting. His father and I told him that giving up was not an option and encouraged him to take the test again. Fortunately, there were others who proved to be a great support system and they encouraged Reggie to keep trying as well. Our collective efforts proved worthwhile, for at last Reggie had passed the test for the first and second parts! His success over this hurdle brought great joy and jubilation to Reggie as well as the rest of the family. No one would have ever guessed that playing basketball all those years would have such an impact on Reggie's adult life. The discipline and perseverance the game taught, along with the push and support of his family circle is what I truly believe aided my son in overcoming his challenges. I believe that is why I truly enjoyed the game I went to see with Reggie as the coach. The boys played with so much intensity and enthusiasm. After the game, two of the parents approached me and asked me how I did it. Confused by their question, I inquired, "How to do *what*?" They immediately replied almost in unison, "How did you get him to be so independent?" Before I could say anything, both parents said their sons were eighteen and they would have to leave home so they could learn to be independent. To their apparent alarm, I informed them that I did not agree with their perspective. "Because an individual has reached eighteen years of age does not automatically make them be independent." I continued. I also stated that my opinion on the matter will remain that parents have to encourage and support their children and make sure they have been trained or educated in some area themselves. I told the parents that Reggie is thirty-two years old and if he wanted to further his education, he could always come home and wouldn't be forced to pay rent or essentials. As a hard of hearing/deaf person, they already have enough challenges as it is without being burdened by some bills that you could help prevent. I encouraged them to allow their sons to get equipped for life so they could become as independent as Reggie is now.

VI.

When It All Comes Together

Reggie received a provisional certificate to teach Math. He teaches Math at the Atlanta School for the Deaf which is a great accomplishment. In fact, while this book is being published, Reggie is wearing several hats. He is the Athletic Director, Varsity Basketball Coach and Math Teacher for the Atlanta Area School for the Deaf. He certainly wants to make a difference in the lives of Deaf people, especially students. Despite the fact that during his elementary, high school, and college years, Reggie fought hard against our promptings to cultivate a more solid reading habit, his life has completely changed for the better-academically for himself, as well as for the students he teach. He overcame his biggest hurdle of acquiring the desire to read, and developed a passion that superseded even my own expectations. I wasn't taken aback, however, when Reggie informed me and my husband that he had enrolled at Valdosta State University in pursuit of his Master's degree in Deaf Education. His passion to teach and cultivate the minds of our nation's youth inspires me to this day! His passion also made him an ideal role model to the Deaf and hearing impaired students he is privileged to teach and nurture-past, present and future.

Sitting here in my teal outfit, adorned with the shiniest gold accessories, my mind wandered again. I didn't realize it until I heard my eldest daughter, Beverly, calling my name as my nieces were being introduced to some of the guests. I smiled broadly as I made eye contact with their beautiful bronze faces, but my thoughts were far from the event that was planned to celebrate my own accomplishments. My eyes darted beyond the groups of family and friends who had gathered that Saturday afternoon in July, shifting from the now crowded room and the entrance several yards away. There was one attendee that my heart was set on greeting that afternoon, yet he had not arrived yet. Once again my thoughts strayed to Reggie. I knew he would come to my retirement party to help his mother celebrate, however, I also realized the strain the whole ordeal would be for him. In hindsight, I truly believe that one of Reggie's biggest regrets was that he did not want his family to learn sign language while he was young. Determined to remain an integral part of his development and growth, I decided against his request and learned how to sign a little. Looking back, I wish I had done more on my own to master that feat. If for no other reason, at least my son would not feel alone amongst family. Frustrated with the fact that he finds it extremely difficult to keep up with what everyone is saying, Reggie made it a practice to distance himself from family gatherings. When Reggie was growing up, I carried him to all family functions. Once he became an adult, he stopped going. Reggie would always come the next day expecting me to tell him what was transpired at the event. He was very uncomfortable because he couldn't laugh with everyone else. He had to laugh after everyone else had already enjoyed a joke. It was significant for those in the Deaf community, not to be singled out or looked upon as being different. On one occasion, Reggie explained to me that when he is with the Deaf community, they usually sit in a circle. This will allow everyone to see who is engaged in the conversation and everyone knows what is being said in the conversation.

Freeing myself from my thoughts, I hear someone in the crowd of family members greet him by name. My eyes still did not bear witness to his face, but I was still searching. A deep breath later, Reggie's round face emerges from the crowd. A former co-worker is speaking to me, but all I see is the smile on my son's face. I'm oblivious to her words, yet my inattentiveness is masked by my polite smile. "He's here!" I whispered under my breath as I exhaled my anxieties away. I understood that this setting would prove uncomfortable for my handsome son, but he would never let his dear mother down. Recently moving out on his own, any occasion I was blessed to spend time around my son was cherished. Now I could relax and enjoy the festivities so carefully planned by my loved ones. I was honored that evening with speeches, roasts, dances, and great food, but one of the biggest honors was being surrounded by all of my children. As I watched the fruits of my labor shuffle around that Saturday, all of the sacrifices made and all of the tears cried throughout the years, seemed very much worthwhile. Melba, my youngest daughter, approached the table where I was seated. “Your former co-workers want to take a picture with you, Mama,” she whispered into my ear in hopes of being audible amidst the singing from the crowd that accompanied the loud music playing in the reception hall. Excusing myself from my dinner guests seated with me at the beautifully adorned head table, I followed Melba to the area in the foyer where my presence was being awaited. Shuffling through the crowds, I peered and smiled. I was looking for Reggie’s face. Surely, he would not have left without saying goodbye to his mama. Reaching the patiently waiting friends who were standing near the doorway, I noticed the back of my son’s head. Smiling to myself, I nodded with approval. He had made the occasion as expected after all, and that was good enough for me. Everyone knew the crowds would overwhelm him with everyone telling jokes and speaking too fast for him to comprehend the reason why those standing near were tearing while bursting with laughter. Yes, I fully understood how isolated that would make Reggie feel. “I love you, son,” I muttered under my breath as I held in my stomach as the flash took our photo.

This book is my personal testimony and the fruition of my love, caring and labor for Reggie. I am so blessed and very appreciative that I lived to see him become self-sufficient in all of his endeavors that he might want to achieve. My influence is ***REGGIE BESS.***

VII.

Appendix

"The Silent Player"

Reggie was the first member of our family to be diagnosed as hard of hearing, which did not hinder his success. In fact, this may have been his motivator to reach some of his goals. He received many awards through the years, including several prestigious awards. He has achieved a Bachelor's Degree in Accounting and a minor in Mathematics and a Master's Degree in Deaf Education.

Here are some of the awards Reggie received while growing up.

The following are clips from the program for Career Day when Reggie was one of the motivational speakers. Below are a few of the letters from some of the students that participated in the program.

Career Day!

"CAREER DAY"
Freedom Middle School

Deaf H/H Students
MAY 6, 2011

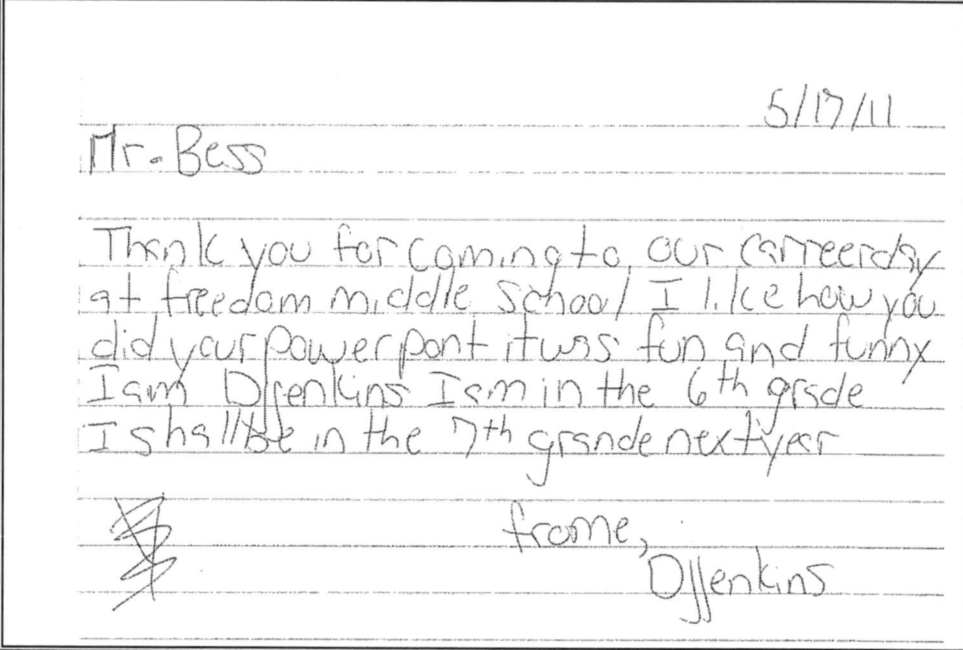

5/17/11

Mr. Bess

Thank you for coming to our careerday at freedom middle School I like how you did your powerpont it was fun and funny I am DJJenkins I am in the 6th grade I shall be in the 7th grande next year

frome,
DJJenkins

****

Mr. Bess

Thank you for coming to "Career Day" at Freedom Middle School. I am in the 7th gr. Next year I will be in the 8th gr. I enjoyed your powerpoint of your life. I will read many books

Thank you

Stephen Fraser

Mrs.Bess

Thank you for coming Freedom Middle School career Day
I am in 7th grade. Next year I will be 8th grade
Next year I will be 8th grade I will do all work
and Homework. I enjoyed your powerpoint

Thank you, Johnquavise Ratliff

Mr. Bess

Thank you for coming to "Career Day" at Freedom Middle School. My name is Kushal Neupane. I am in the 7th grade. You taught me how to become a better student and get good grades.

Thank you,

Kushal Neupane

The Manual Alphabet and "I Love You" Sign

About The Author

Born in Griffin, Georgia, Lavonia Lusier-Bess currently resides in Union City, Georgia enjoying retirement with her husband William (Bill) Bess, Sr. With a strong love for youth, Lavonia spends her free time as an advocate and supporter of higher education.

The Bess Family

(From Left to right): Lavonia Bess, Beverly, Lil' Bill, Melba, Reggie, Bill Bess Sr.

Made in the USA
Columbia, SC
24 March 2025

55643725R00050